everyday STEM

MATH

MATH IN ACTION

Numbers and shapes are all around you

KINGFISHER
LONDON & NEW YORK

First published 2024 in the United States by Kingfisher
120 Broadway, New York, NY 10271
Kingfisher is an imprint of Macmillan Children's Books, London
All rights reserved.

Copyright © Macmillan Publishers International Ltd. 2024

ISBN: 978-0-7534-8026-7

Distributed in the U.S. and Canada by Macmillan,
120 Broadway, New York, NY 10271

Library of Congress Cataloging-in-Publication data has been applied for.

Author: Lou Abercrombie
Illustrator: Evelyn Rogers
Series editor: Lizzie Davey
Series design: Jim Green

Kingfisher Books are available for special promotions and premiums.
For details contact:
Special Markets Department, Macmillan
120 Broadway, New York, NY 10271.

For more information please visit:
www.kingfisherbooks.com

Printed in China

9 8 7 6 5 4 3 2 1
1TR/0124/WKT/UG/128MA

EU representative: Macmillan Publishers Ireland Ltd, 1st Floor,
The Liffey Trust Centre, 117-126 Sheriff Street Upper, Dublin 1, D01 YC43

FSC
www.fsc.org
MIX
Paper | Supporting
responsible forestry
FSC® C116313

CONTENTS

THE ART OF MATH

Math is the science of numbers and shapes, and applied math is what we do with them. This could mean solving real life problems using calculation, estimating outcomes using probability and statistics, or using measurement to build things. But you don't have to be a mathematician to use math—everyone uses it! This includes teachers, accountants, doctors, engineers, sports people, and even artists. So how does math factor in to an art exhibition?

Technology
Cameras, phones, electronic guides, electronic tracking systems, Wi-Fi, and security are the results of algebra, calculus, probability, geometry, and trigonometry at work. QR codes and Wi-Fi tracking can tell a museum how many people have visited a particular exhibit, while electronic barcodes can monitor what people spend in the gift shop.

Design
Ever wondered why paintings are hung at a particular height, or why benches are put a certain distance away from a piece of art? What about the suggested route through a museum, or the layout of a certain room? It's carefully designed, thanks to geometry, trigonometry, and measurement.

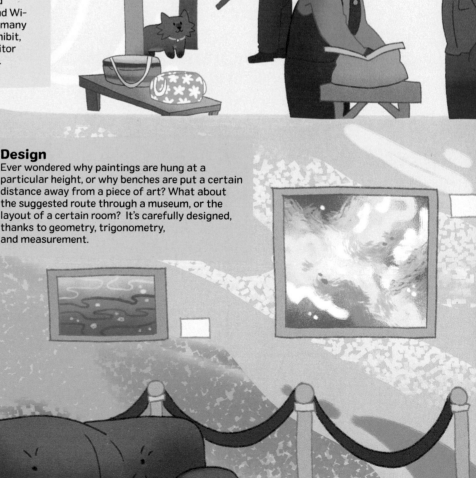

Art

Artists use measurement to estimate proportion, angles, and lines for distance, while the rules of composition (the art of arranging things in a frame) make sure images are pleasing to the eye. Modern artists even use data to create art!

Business success

How successful is an exhibit? How many visitors can safely fit in at once? What sells well? These questions that determine a business's success can be assessed using probability and statistics via surveys, barcodes, and electronic tracking systems.

M. C. ESCHER (1898–1972)

Maurits Cornelis Escher was a Dutch graphic artist. He had no formal training in mathematics beyond high school but is widely admired by mathematicians for his ability to show mathematical principles in his art. Escher explored patterns and tessellations (arrangements of closed shapes) and was fascinated with how shapes changed and interacted with each other.

Escher's Flying Fish

WHAT ARE THE CHANCES?

Being certain about the possibility of something happening is both reassuring and helpful when making decisions. But often we can't know something for certain. This is the case in all kinds of circumstances. For example, will a business be successful? Will it rain tomorrow? When we don't know the answers, we can make educated guesses based on what we do know. This is where probability and statistics come in.

Probability is the science of chance. It expresses how likely something is and is written in fractions, decimals, or percentages. Probability is essential in our daily lives, including for weather forecasting, estimating financial results, and predicting medical outcomes.

THE PROBABILITY SCALE

The Probability Scale is a way of showing the likelihood of something happening. It ranges from certain (1, or 100% likely) to even (½, or 50:50 chances), and then impossible (0, no chance it would ever happen!). Here are a few examples of likelihoods.

1
CERTAIN

½
EVEN

0
IMPOSSIBLE

Certain
There are two sides to a coin (100%).

Very likely
Two people at a party of 75 will share a birthday (99%).

Likely
The probability of picking a number from 2 to 10 in a deck of cards (36/52 or 69%)

Even chance
You get tails when a coin is tossed (50%).

Unlikely
The odds of you rolling a 1 or 2 on a die are 2 in 6 (33%).

Very unlikely
The card you pick is an ace (4 in 52 chance, or 7.7%).

Impossible
The magician can pull a unicorn out of their hat!

OUTCOMES

The probability of an event is assessed by counting the different possible outcomes. Events that cannot happen at the same time are "mutually exclusive," while events that can occur at the same time are "non-mutually exclusive."

MUTUALLY EXCLUSIVE EVENTS

These are when two or more events cannot happen at the same time. For example, you can't roll a 1 and a 5 in a single roll of a die; you can't get a head and a tail in a single toss of a coin; and you can't turn left and right at the same time!

NON-MUTUALLY EXCLUSIVE EVENTS

When events share common outcomes, they are called non-mutually exclusive. To make it even more complex, these outcomes can further be classified into being dependent or independent.

INDEPENDENT EVENTS

The outcome of the first event doesn't influence the outcome of the second. For example, what's the probability of tossing a head followed by a tail?

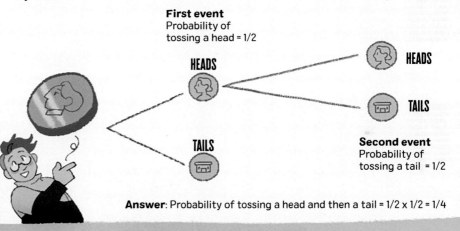

First event
Probability of tossing a head = 1/2

HEADS

HEADS

TAILS

TAILS

Second event
Probability of tossing a tail = 1/2

Answer: Probability of tossing a head and then a tail = 1/2 x 1/2 = 1/4

DID YOU KNOW?

If you shuffle a pack of cards thoroughly, it is likely that the exact order of the cards in the pack has never been seen before. Ever!

DEPENDENT EVENTS

The outcome of an event is affected by the outcome of another. For example, from a set of five cards, what's the probability of picking a yellow card and then a blue card, from a set of five different colored cards?

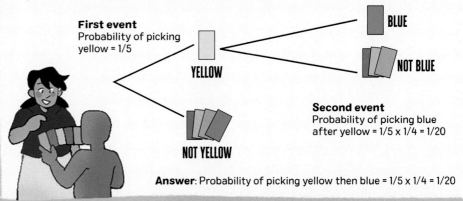

First event
Probability of picking yellow = 1/5

BLUE

NOT BLUE

YELLOW

NOT YELLOW

Second event
Probability of picking blue after yellow = 1/5 x 1/4 = 1/20

Answer: Probability of picking yellow then blue = 1/5 x 1/4 = 1/20

UNDERSTANDING DATA

In the competitive world of business, companies must make sound decisions to safeguard their success. Data about their customers can help businesses spot trends, drive revenue, ensure staying power, and improve their services and products. Statistics are an invaluable tool in this decision-making process. By collecting data from surveys, studies, and experiments, we can summarize and display these numbers in graphic form for analysis and interpretation.

MARKET RESEARCH

Market research is the collection and presentation of data. It enables businesses to better understand their industry and may give them the edge over competitors.

FIELD RESEARCH

This is information that is gathered out and about. It involves . . .

- Online surveys
- Face-to-face feedback
- Focus groups—people brought together to discuss products or ideas.

DESK RESEARCH

This is the information we gather from our desks. It involves . . .

- Analyzing sales data
- Understanding website use
- QR codes
- Newspaper and magazine articles
- Social media

QR code matrix example

QR CODES

Quick Response (QR) codes are two-dimensional barcodes composed of a unique arrangement of squares called a matrix. Their usefulness goes two ways. For the customer, it's an easy way to get online information. For the business, it allows them to track the data of the customer.

IT'S ALL IN THE PRESENTATION

When it comes to analyzing data, success is all about presentation. It is important to make information eye-catching and easy to understand. Choosing the right graph to display your data is key to helping a business bloom.

"Beautiful flowers!"

PICTOGRAM

These use repeated images to represent simple data. They are often used to make boring information look more interesting.

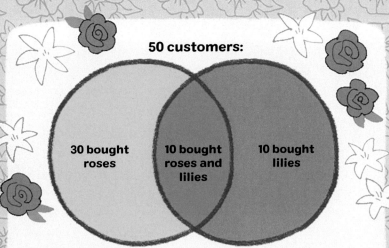

50 customers:

30 bought roses | 10 bought roses and lilies | 10 bought lilies

VENN DIAGRAM

This is a series of circles in which the overlapping sections represent similarities. Businesses use Venn diagrams to make comparisons.

TALLY CHARTS

Tallies are used to collect data quickly and effectively. Each fifth line is drawn across the previous four.

Favorite flower	Number of people
Rose	卌 III
Lily	卌 II
Daffodil	卌 IIII
Gerbera	卌 IIII
Carnation	II
Peony	卌 卌 II

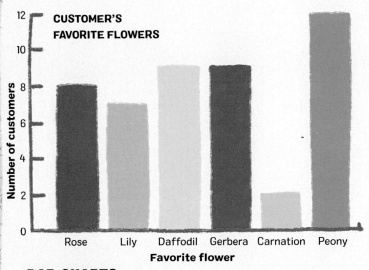

CUSTOMER'S FAVORITE FLOWERS

BAR CHARTS

Bar charts allow businesses to compare amounts. The same information could be drawn on a line graph as plotted points and lines.

PIE CHARTS

These charts show us proportion. They can tell a business about things like customer preference and spending habits, or when to expect seasonal spikes.

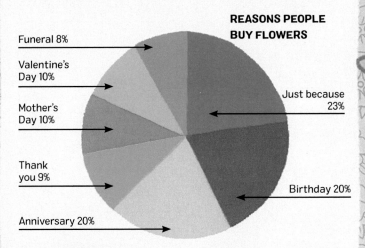

REASONS PEOPLE BUY FLOWERS

Funeral 8%
Valentine's Day 10%
Mother's Day 10%
Thank you 9%
Anniversary 20%
Just because 23%
Birthday 20%

THE PRISONER'S DILEMMA

Statistics play a major role in psychology, in which data is invaluable to experimental design. The Prisoner's Dilemma was created by mathematician Albert Tucker to see how people cooperate (or not). It works like this:

Prisoners **A** and **B** have been charged with committing a crime together and are in separate cells. Each has the chance to confess. Neither knows what the other will choose to do.

The possible outcomes are as follows:
1. If only one prisoner confesses, that prisoner is set free, but the other prisoner serves three years in prison.
2. If neither prisoner confesses, they will both serve one year in prison.
3. If both prisoners confess, both will serve two years.

A SPOONFUL OF NUMBERS

Mathematics can be lifesaving. It plays a crucial role in medicine, answering questions such as "How effective is a new drug?" "What is the survival rate of a particular procedure?" "Which treatment plan is right?" Any medical decision must be backed up by evidence. This is where probability and statistics come in. By interpreting medical research, we can predict outcomes for better rates of success.

Should Prisoner **A** keep quiet or betray Prisoner **B** and admit to the crime?

What would you do?

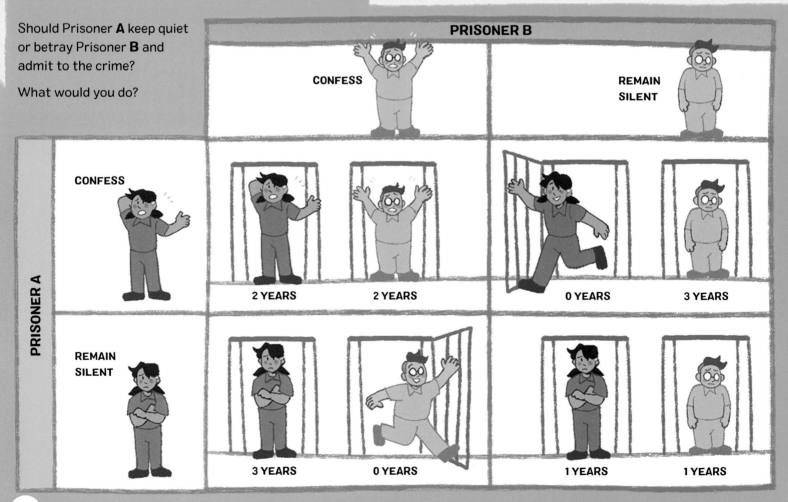

PRISONER B

PRISONER A

CONFESS | REMAIN SILENT

CONFESS: 2 YEARS | 2 YEARS | 0 YEARS | 3 YEARS

REMAIN SILENT: 3 YEARS | 0 YEARS | 1 YEARS | 1 YEARS

THE RELIABILITY OF TESTING

Not all medical tests are accurate. In these cases, we look at plausibility—how likely something is to happen, based on other things already having happened. The formula we use to do this, called Bayes Theorem, is the most applied formula in science:

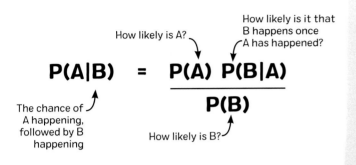

How likely is A?

How likely is it that B happens once A has happened?

$$P(A|B) = \frac{P(A)\ P(B|A)}{P(B)}$$

The chance of A happening, followed by B happening

How likely is B?

MISLEADING STATISTICS

Did you know 76.5% of children love candy? Actually, that's not true; it's a made-up number! But it goes to show how easily people believe a narrative when it is presented as a statistic. Unfortunately, the misrepresentation of data, either intentionally or by error, happens regularly when people want to prove their point.

FLORENCE NIGHTINGALE (1820–1910)

Florence Nightingale was a nurse and statistician. During the Crimean War (1854-1856), she organized a team of nurses to treat the many soldiers suffering in military hospitals. Florence made it her mission to improve cleanliness standards. In doing so, she cut the hospital's death rate by two-thirds. Her approach as a statistician was methodical, with the patients' data recorded in tables. She was part of a Royal Commission into the health of the army, which discovered that most deaths were caused by preventable diseases and not battle. Her insistence on hand washing has been proven by science and is still essential today.

WASH YOUR HANDS!

Florence Nightingale was also guilty of tweaking her numbers to help her fight her cause. She created a "Rose diagram" instead of using a bar chart. It implied that her arrival at the hospital changed everything when in fact, the number of deaths had already been falling for some months. Two circles are divided into twelve wedges show the number of annual deaths each month. Blue represents deaths caused by disease; red shows deaths by battle wounds; and black means other reasons.

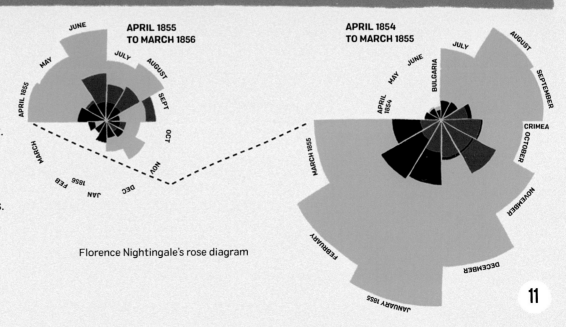

APRIL 1855 TO MARCH 1856

APRIL 1854 TO MARCH 1855

Florence Nightingale's rose diagram

THE MATH WE PLAY

Game theory uses probability and statistics to study the behavior of two or more parties. Used to analyze conflict and strategy, it helps us understand how and why people make decisions. This ability to predict the way our rivals will act in a given situation is useful across many spheres, including politics and business. It is also handy in games, including sports, puzzles, board games, game shows, and video games.

LOGICAL THINKING

Originating in India 1,500 years ago, chess is a game of logic that simulates a battle between two kingdoms. The notations used to describe chess moves are based on a system of coordinates. Players' strengths—based on past matches—are presented as statistics, while probability is used for strategy, such as which opening move to make.

THE MONTY HALL PROBLEM

You're on a game show. Behind one of the doors is a prize. You pick the yellow door. The game show host (who knows where the prize is) picks red and opens it to reveal there's nothing there. You're then given the chance to switch to green. Should you?

The answer, which is somewhat counterintuitive and has baffled many mathematicians, is you should always switch. Why? Because there's a 1/3 chance when you pick the yellow door, meaning there's a 2/3 chance of the prize being behind the other two doors. When the game show host opens the red door (which they know doesn't have the prize), that 2/3 probability moves entirely onto the green door.

ZERO-SUM GAMES

A zero-sum game is a win-lose scenario between two sides, where if one sides wins, the other side loses, and vice-versa. Games like tennis and soccer are zero-sum games. For example, in a penalty kick, either the kicker scores the goal (win) or the goal is missed or prevented (lose). This is also another example of strategy, as both the goalkeeper and the kicker must decide their moves simultaneously, before knowing what the other has decided.

Which way to shoot?

Which way to dive?

How much do we know? How much do they know?

How much do we know? How much do they know?

DO I KNOW THAT YOU KNOW WHAT I KNOW…?

Team sports are about strategy—trying to guess your opponent's tactics and making plans on how to tackle them to win. By using probabilities to understand the strengths of a particular team or player, coaches can estimate outcomes based on past performances, determine what areas the team is already strong in, and decide where they need to focus their practice.

JOB: VIDEO GAME DESIGNER

As well as being creative, able to meet deadlines and communicate well, and be a team player, video game designers must be good at math. Problem solving and programming skills are needed for game mechanics, character design, narrative and plot, level design, and core game concept, as well as coding, debugging, and testing. Getting a game's balance right between luck and strategy comes down to game theory and probability.

THE CHANCES OF RAIN

Being able to predict the weather is very useful. It makes you less likely to get caught in a sudden downpour and helps you decide when to visit the beach! More important, being able to assess the likelihood of dangerous weather conditions helps save lives—extreme weather, such as tornadoes and hurricanes, can have devastating effects. Weather forecasting uses probability and statistics to help scientists make predictions about what the weather is likely to be.

Meteorology is the science of studying weather. "Weather" means the conditions in Earth's atmosphere at a particular point. This includes temperature, cloudiness, wind strength, and how much moisture is in the air.

HOW TO FORECAST THE WEATHER

1. Take a snapshot of Earth's whole atmosphere at a particular time.

2. Feed your observations and measurements into a powerful computer, to simulate the current weather conditions.

3. Step the model forward in time, to create a new snapshot of what the weather could be like in the future.

4. Study the data and turn it into a meaningful forecast.

CHAOS!

No weather forecast is 100% accurate. Why? Because the atmosphere is a chaotic system: there are 2×10^{44} molecules in the air, moving around randomly. No computer model could ever represent them all! To help weather centers gain more confidence in their uncertainty, they often perform multiple slightly different runs of their weather models.

CHAOS THEORY

If a butterfly flaps its wings in India, does the tiny change in air pressure set off a tornado in Texas? This simple metaphor is known as the Butterfly Effect. It is used to explain chaos theory: the idea that a small, insignificant event could have much larger consequences elsewhere.

THE LANGUAGE OF WEATHER

Statistics help us analyze, summarize, and present findings from a collection of data. They are a useful tool when talking about the weather, as they can help us decide things such as when and where to go on vacation. Here are some examples of words we use to describe statistics.

MEDIAN—the number in the middle of a list of numbers, when they are put in order from smallest to largest.

MODE—the number that appears the most times in a data set.

MEAN—the average number in a data set, found by adding all the numbers then dividing by how many numbers there are.

RANGE—the difference between the biggest and smallest numbers in a set of data.

DESCRIBING CHANCES

Forecasters use particular words to talk about the probability of rainfall. Anything above 70% is a "high" chance.

Forecast terminology	Probability of precipitation	Descriptive words used
—	Less than 20%	Drizzle, sprinkle (flurries)
Slight chance	20%	Isolated
Chance	30–50%	Scattered
Likely	60–70%	Numerous

MEASURING RAIN

The words used to describe amounts of rainfall have very specific meanings.

Word used	Rainfall rate
Very light	< 0.01 inch per hour
Light	0.01 to 0.1 inch per hour
Moderate	0.1 to 0.3 inches per hour
Heavy	> 0.3 inches per hour

Today

	Thursday	Friday	Saturday	Sunday	Monday
35° 27°	**38°** 31°	**36°** 31°	**38°** 29°	**37°** 33°	

Gentle rain and a breeze

12 p.m.	1 p.m.	2 p.m.	3 p.m.	4 p.m.	5 p.m.	6 p.m.	7 p.m.	8 p.m.	9 p.m.
									35°
33°	**33°**	**33°**	**33°**	**33°**	**33°**	**33°**	**33°**	**33°**	
50%	88%	78%	84%	89%	90%	90%	86%	85%	80%

THE PROBABILITY OF PRECIPITATION

Weather forecasts need to tell us what level of confidence the forecasters have in their predictions, especially when it comes to rain (or snow). This is done using percentages.

The percentage can be calculated using this formula:

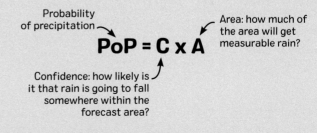

Probability of precipitation

Area: how much of the area will get measurable rain?

$$PoP = C \times A$$

Confidence: how likely is it that rain is going to fall somewhere within the forecast area?

Example: If C = 30% (0.3) and A = 70% (0.7), then PoP = 0.3 x 0.7 = 0.21 or 21%. In other words, there's a 21% chance of rain at that time for that location.

NOTHING TO SEE HERE!

One of the most important discoveries in the evolution of mathematics was nothing at all. Literally! Because if there was nothing to count, then why try to count it? Many ancient civilizations developed their own number systems, including the Egyptians, Mayans, and Sumerians. They had math, but it had one major limitation: the lack of a zero.

THANKS FOR NOTHING

With zero as a placeholder, mathematicians can work with very large numbers. Some of them are so large that they can't easily be written down.

Take the Googolplex. In 1920, nine-year-old Milton Sirotta, the nephew of mathematician Edward Kasner, named the number 10^{100} as a "googol." He then suggested the term "googolplex," meaning "one, followed by writing zeros until you get tired" or 10googol (that's 1 followed by a googol of zeros) .

In 2013, Wolfgang H. Nitsche published *Googolplex Written Out*. It took him 10,000,000,000,000,000,000,000,000,000,000,000,000,000,000,000,000,000,000,000,000,000,000,000,000,000,000,000,000,000,000,000,000,000,000,000,000,000 volumes of the book to do it (that's 94 zeros).

WHY DO WE NEED ZERO?

As a **placeholder**: counting is about recording the number of ones, tens, hundreds, thousands, and so on. Without zero, there's no way of telling the difference between numbers.

1   10   50   90

As a **place value**: every digit in a number also represents an amount, based on its position. Zero is also an amount.

Hundreds	Tens	Ones
1	0	6

FINDING NOTHING

Across eight centuries several Indian mathematicians fine-tuned the concept of zero, helping create the positional "Hindu-Arabic" number system that we use today.

ARYABATHA OF KUSUMUPURA (476-550) was an Indian mathematician and astronomer, often considered to be the greatest genius of all time. He discovered that the Moon shines because of the reflection of the Sun. He also invented the decimal system with place value, and used the concept of zero (as the word kha) in his work.

BRAHMAGUPTA (600-680) was the first person to use zero as a number and write it as a circle.

It was **MAHAVIRA (800-870)** who indicated that the multiplication of zero by any number is zero.

Finally, **BHASKARA II (1114-1185)** determined that any number divided by zero indicates an infinite quantity. He is also responsible for proposing a way of solving quadratic equations in which $ax^2 + bx + c = 0$.

1x1

THE EVOLUTION OF A NUMBER SYSTEM

In the Middle Ages, Europe launched a series of military invasions into the Middle East—the Crusades. One result of the Crusades was that Muslim scholars, including Al-Uqlidisi (920-980), taught European scholars about science and medicine, and introduced them to the number system that is used around the world today.

Brahmi		—	=	≡	+	И	ℓ	ງ	Ƨ	Ɂ
Hindu	○	۶	२	३	४	५	६	७	८	९
Arabic	•	١	٢	٣	٤	٥	٦	٧	٨	٩
Medieval	O	I	2	3	Ջ	Ɠ	6	ʌ	8	9
Modern	**0**	**1**	**2**	**3**	**4**	**5**	**6**	**7**	**8**	**9**

THE LENGTHS WE GO TO

Have you ever thought about math before diving into a swimming pool? Well, someone has! All sorts of math goes into swimming, from the length and mass required to calculate the volume and weight of the water, to the height of a diving board and the depth of the deep end, and timekeeping for Olympic swimming records. All of this splashing around potential is thanks to metrology (measurement), geometry, and trigonometry.

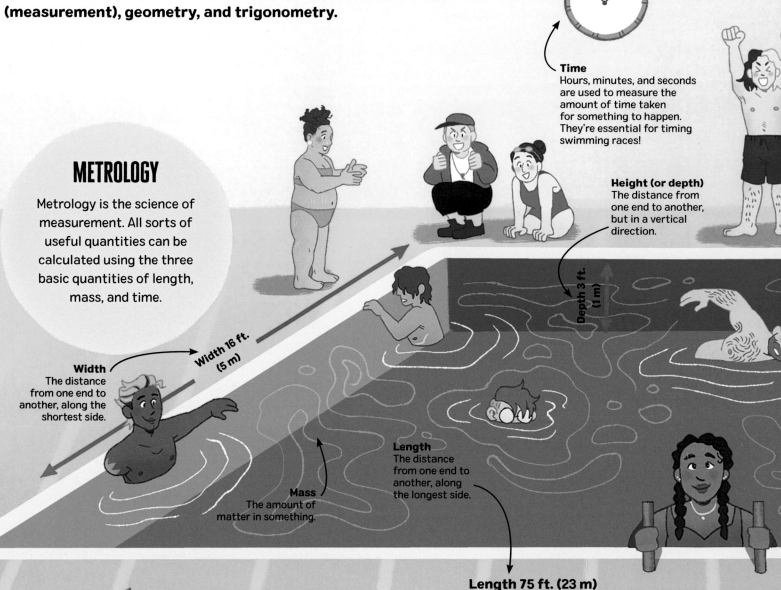

Time
Hours, minutes, and seconds are used to measure the amount of time taken for something to happen. They're essential for timing swimming races!

METROLOGY

Metrology is the science of measurement. All sorts of useful quantities can be calculated using the three basic quantities of length, mass, and time.

Height (or depth)
The distance from one end to another, but in a vertical direction.

Depth 3 ft. (1 m)

Width
The distance from one end to another, along the shortest side.

Width 16 ft. (5 m)

Mass
The amount of matter in something.

Length
The distance from one end to another, along the longest side.

Length 75 ft. (23 m)

TRIGONOMETRY

Trigonometry is the math of triangles. Right-angle triangles have specific relationships between their angles and lengths. We can using the special ratios of sine, cosine, and tangent to figure out any missing angles and distances.

$$\text{Sin } x = \frac{\text{Opposite}}{\text{Hypotenuse}}$$

$$\text{Cos } x = \frac{\text{Adjacent}}{\text{Hypotenuse}}$$

$$\text{Tan } x = \frac{\text{Opposite}}{\text{Adjacent}}$$

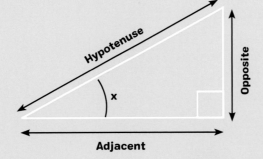

DIVING IN

The moment of entry is important for a competitive swimmer's dive start. After pushing off horizontally through the air, a swimmer will aim for a 30° entry angle.

$$\tan 30^0 = 0.577 = \frac{5 \text{ ft.}}{a}$$

$$\text{Therefore } a = \frac{5}{0.577} = 8.67 \text{ ft.}$$

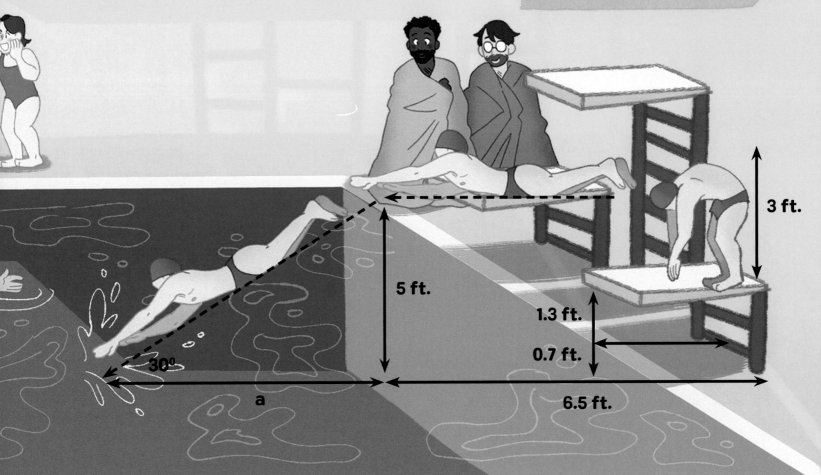

TRAVELING IN TIME

Where would we be without time? Probably late! Being able to tell time and figure out how long things take is incredibly useful. Without time, we wouldn't know whether we were coming or going! Think about going on vacation. The travel industry is all about time-tabling and scheduling. That includes getting people from A to B, securing them accommodation for the right week, and booking them on excursions.

ABOUT TIME!

Have you ever felt like time is dragging when you're bored, or how quickly it seems to fly when you're having fun? Really, we are all traveling through time at exactly the same speed: 1 second per second. Is time travel possible? Well, we can't go back in time, but we do know that a year goes by 15 milliseconds faster at the top of Mount Everest than it does at sea level. This is because time goes by more slowly if you are closer to Earth.

DID YOU KNOW?

Jet lag is worse when traveling from west to east. Physicists have used a mathematical model to prove that it's easier to lengthen our day by flying west than it is to shorten it by flying east.

JUST A SECOND

One second is 1/60 of a minute, or 1/3,600 of an hour. But the division of time doesn't stop there! A jiffy is an actual unit of time: 1/100 of a second. A quectosecond is one nonillionth of a second (that's 10^{-30}), and Planck time is the smallest measurable time span: 10^{-43} of a second.

JET LAG

Did you know that you have an internal body clock? Using daylight, temperature, and hormones, our circadian rhythm tells our bodies when to wake and sleep over a 24-hour period. Unfortunately, moving between time zones ruins this routine. It can cause "jet lag," which has symptoms such as headache and insomnia.

TIME ZONES

Daytime is defined as the period between sunrise and sunset, while nighttime is the period of darkness when the Sun lights up the other side of the world. To deal with these global time differences, we use imaginary lines that run between the North and South Poles. They divide the world into 24 time zones, each representing one hour of the day.

Large countries such as Australia and the United States have many time zones, while smaller countries usually have just one.

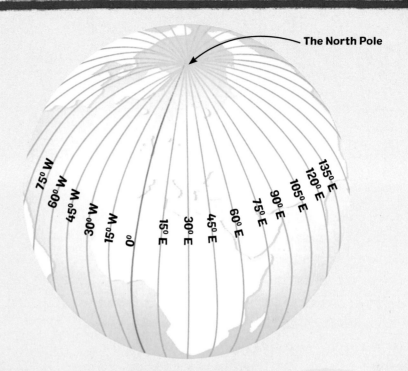

The North Pole

75° W
60° W
45° W
30° W
15° W
0°
15° E
30° E
45° E
60° E
75° E
90° E
105° E
120° E
135° E

HERE COMES THE SUN

The first clocks were sundials, which tracked the movement of an object's shadow. The people who first made these lived in the Northern Hemisphere, so the first clocks with hands moved in the same direction as the shadow: clockwise.

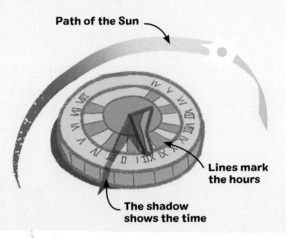

Path of the Sun

Lines mark the hours

The shadow shows the time

KEEPING TIME

Before time zones were created, towns kept their own time by setting their clocks to local solar noon. This made it difficult (and dangerous!) to schedule trains between different places. Eventually, train companies across the U.S., Canada, and the U.K. began using a standardized system to regulate their schedules.

WARNING:
Never look directly at the Sun.

HOW TO TELL TIME

You can tell time using your own hands! On a clear day, find the Sun and hold your hand in front of you so that your little finger is parallel with the horizon. Put your other hand on top of the first, then move the first hand on top of the second, then repeat until you reach the Sun. The time until sunset is the number of hands and fingers between horizon and Sun. Each finger stands for 15 minutes, so four fingers equal an hour.

WRITTEN IN THE STARS

Years before compasses or GPS were invented, people found their way around by looking up at the sky. Some ancient civilizations kept track of the movements of the planets, believing this would help them predict the future. Others used the Sun's movement to understand direction. Early astronomers realized that stars are constants in the night sky. They may appear to move as Earth rotates, but their positions and alignment with other stars never changes.

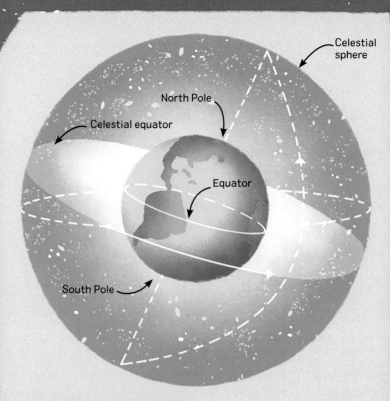

Celestial sphere

North Pole

Celestial equator

Equator

South Pole

THE CELESTIAL SPHERE

The celestial sphere is an imagined surface around Earth. By thinking of it as a real sphere at an infinite distance from our planet, with Earth at its center, we can establish coordinates on it. These are used to mark the positions of stars and planets.

MEASURING THE SKY

Astronomers use angles, arc minutes ('), and arc seconds (") when measuring the sky. The "angular distance" of an object is measured by the angular separation between its opposite edges. There are 360° in a circle or sphere, where 1 degree = 60' and 1'= 60'

Angular distance

WANG ZHENYI
(1768–1797)

Wang Zhenyi was one of the most famous female academics of China's Qing dynasty. She believed that women should work to their fullest potential, despite the customs of the time, which stopped girls from getting an education. Zhenyi did experiments at home, studying the movement of the Sun, Moon, and planets. She showed how lunar and solar eclipses worked using a round table as Earth, a lamp as the Sun, and a mirror as the Moon. She wrote books on astronomy, math, and poetry.

WOMEN ARE EQUAL TO MEN—AREN'T YOU CONVINCED THAT DAUGHTERS CAN ALSO BE HEROIC?

Zenith point

Vertical

Complete circle = 360°

Semi circle = 180°

90°

Horizon

FINDING YOUR ZENITH

Imagine you are the center of your own celestial sphere. If we think of the top half of the sky as a semicircle (180°), with the ground as the dividing line, then the other half (below the horizon) is out of sight. Now stick your hand straight above your head, perpendicular to the horizon. This is the zenith point, which is 90° from the horizon.

MEET THE MEASURERS

There's a real art to getting design right. Everything that has been designed has math behind it, including architecture, landscape gardening, illustration, art, and much more! Everyone who works in one of these areas uses math and numbers in some form, whether it's measurement for scale and proportion or angles for determining symmetry.

LANDSCAPE GARDENERS

To create a new garden, landscape gardeners first survey the plot to get accurate measurements for their designs. To do this, they use scale. Scale enables them to produce a smaller version of the garden on paper. A scale of 1:36 means that every 1 in. on a drawing represents 36 in. (1 yd.) in the garden.

ARCHITECTS

Architects use a whole range of measurement to ensure symmetry, balance, and structurally sound designs for their buildings. One of the ways they do this is by using the relationships between different angles. Here are a few examples:

Corresponding angles ensure the symmetry and balance of a design.

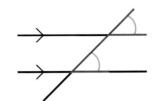

Alternate interior angles are on the opposite sides of a line crossing two parallel lines, but on the inside. They are used to ensure that parts of buildings are parallel.

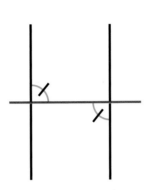

ARTISTS AND ILLUSTRATORS

Not all art is exact. If you look at Picasso's portraits, you'll see that the proportions of his models are very abstract! However, one thing all artists do consider is whether they have the balance of their picture right, which means using the rules of composition.

That includes:

• Using leading lines that tell the viewer's eyes where to look in the picture.

• Arranging elements within the image carefully, so it's clear which of them are the most important.

• Using scale to give proportion and a sense of size.

One way of arranging a composition is by using the rule of thirds. Dividing a picture into a grid of nine squares produces four central focal points. The general rule is not to cover all four focal points.

SKATEPARK HIGHS AND LOWS

Skateboarding is an extreme sport in which a person stands and balances on a small piece of wood and wheels. It's the union of physics—think gravity, friction, and Newton's third law of motion—engineering, design, and math. Skateboarding can be done anywhere if there's a decent smooth surface, but if you want to explore the vertical possibilities of the sport, you need a skateboard park. And that involves math!

WHAT MAKES A GOOD SKATEPARK?

Skatepark designers use measurement, trigonometry, and geometry when designing a new park. There are safety measures to think about, such as walkways for pedestrians. Most important, they must consider the joy of the ride. This includes making sure there is enough space for groups of skaters to use the park, having plenty of lines to follow between obstacles, and including features that let skaters whiz into the air. Here are a few examples of the math behind top-notch skateboarding ramps.

Pyramid ramps
These ramps are usually four-sided in design. They are shaped like pyramids, but with the top cut off to provide a platform for flat-landing flip tricks.

Wave ramps
These have a continuous rise and fall pattern, starting and ending at ground level. Riding one can feel like surfing. Skaters can learn to control their speed while doing rotating tricks.

Launch ramps
This is the most common type of skatepark ramp. It has a basic slope, with a curve of around 60° or less.

Bowl ramps

Not all bowl ramps are the same—they come in many shapes and sizes, with either a circular or flat base. They are usedful for picking up speed quickly. Shallow bowls are good for less experienced skaters, while bowls with high curvature have the potential for reaching high speeds and launching into the air.

Half-pipe

Half-pipes consist of two one-fourth pipes with two walls and a flat base. The walls reach a peak of 90° and can be from 7 to 14 ft. (2 to 4.3 m) high. Half-pipes are good for building up speed, letting skaters do tricks in the air.

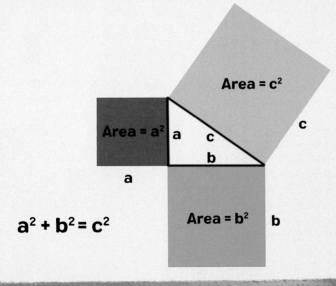

PYTHAG IN ACTION

We want our ramp to be 10 ft. high, with a slope of 15 ft. We can use the Pythagorean theorem to figure out what the bottom length (b) will need to be.

15 ft.

9 ft.

b

PYTHAGOREAN THEOREM

This theorem shows that the square of the length of the hypotenuse of a right triangle is equal to the sum of the squares of the lengths of its other two sides.

Area = c^2

Area = a^2

a

c

b

a

Area = b^2

b

$a^2 + b^2 = c^2$

$$a^2 + b^2 = c^2$$
$$9^2 + b^2 = 15^2$$
$$81 + b^2 = 225$$

Therefore $b^2 = 144$

$$b = \sqrt{144} = 12 \text{ ft.}$$

SOMETHING TO PROVE

Problem solving is a part of our daily lives. This could include calculating how far your budget will go at the grocery store, scaling up a recipe, or calculating how much time you need to bake a cake for a party. Algebra helps us solve these problems by breaking down a problem into a sequence of steps and using letters to represent unknown variables.

TERMS IN ALGEBRA

• A **theorem** is a rule in mathematics, expressed as an equation or formula.

• An **equation** is made up of numbers and letters, called variables, which express the relationship between the different variables when the statements on either side of the equals sign are equal.

For example, a linear equation might look like this:

ax + by = cz

x, y, and z are unknown variables, and a, b, and c are coefficients (known quantities).

• A **formula** is a mathematical rule that is often expressed as an equation. For example, The Pythagorean theorem $a^2 + b^2 = c^2$ is a formula that compares the sides of a right triangle.

• A **proof** is an explanation of why something is true. When you solve an equation, you are providing proof that you have found a value or values that make the two statements equal.

DOUGHNUT EQUATIONS

Let's consider a doughnut recipe that you want to be ready for lunch at noon. Using a linear equation, we can work backward and find out what time you need to start.

Making doughnuts requires:

15 mins. to rest the yeast, sugar, and warm milk while you mix the flour, salt, and sugar

10 min. to add the rest of the ingredients and the yeast mixture

10 min. to knead the dough

45 min. to prove

5 min. to knead the dough again and divide it into balls

30 min. to prove

35 min. to fry

As an equation, this would be:

Total time = yeast + ingredient mix + 1st knead + 1st prove + 2nd knead + 2nd prove + fry time

= 15 + 10 + 10 + 45 + 5 + 30 + 35 min.

= 150 min.

= 2.5 hr.

We know the doughnuts need to be ready by noon, so our start time should be as follows:

12 p.m. – 2.5 hours = 9:30 a.m.

GETTING THE BALANCE RIGHT

When solving equations, it's important that whatever you do to the left-hand side, you also do to the right.

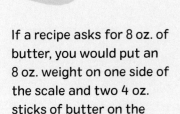

If a recipe asks for 8 oz. of butter, you would put an 8 oz. weight on one side of the scale and two 4 oz. sticks of butter on the other, to make it equal.

$$8 = 4 + 4$$

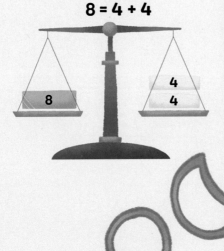

If you were doubling the recipe, you would need to add double to both sides of the scale.

$$2 \times 8 = 2 \times (4 + 4)$$

EMMY NOETHER (1882–1935)

Albert Einstein called German mathematician Emmy Noether the "most significant creative mathematical genius thus far produced since the higher education of women began." However, Noether had much to prove to get there! When she was certified to teach in 1900, women were only allowed to check students' work with the permission of male teachers. By 1915, Noether had a PhD, and her knowledge of algebra earned her an invitation to help other mathematicians explore the math behind Einstein's recent theory on general relativity. However, it wasn't until 1919 that she was given formal permission to be an academic lecturer.

LIGHTS, CAMERA, ALGORITHMS!

Welcome to the movies! Here you can lose yourself in a magical world of action, intrigue, and adventure. But have you ever thought about the math behind what you're watching while you're eating popcorn? Many numbers have been crunched and problems solved. Algebra and calculus play a starring role in bringing animated movies to life, thanks to the parts they play in computer algorithms.

EVERY HOP, SKIP, AND A JUMP!

Computer software is a set of programs and procedures that tell a computer what to do. Coding is the process of creating these instructions, while scripting allows a user to edit a program to perform a specific task. Animators must be able to code and script as well as being able to paint and draw.

For every movement a character makes on screen, two things must happen:

1. The animator draws the main poses a figure might go through to complete the movement.

2. The computer calculates what happens to connect the poses together and make it look like the character is moving smoothly. This is calling splining.

FRAME RATE

Frame rate is the number of frames that appear in a second of film (fps). Film is usually shot at 24 fps, while TV uses 30 fps in the US and 25 fps in Europe. Most video games need much higher frame rates to run smoothly. Things are slightly different for 2D animation, as 24fps would mean drawing a different image 24 times to fill just one second. That's a lot of drawing! If there isn't much action in a 2D film, it's possible to use one drawing for two frames. In some Japanese animation, one drawing might even be used across 4 frames.

During 1 second of film

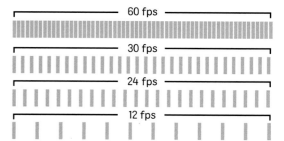

60 fps
30 fps
24 fps
12 fps

The stages of a jump

1. Neutral pose
2. Anticipation
3. Jump (contact pose)
4. Midair pose—at the peak of the jump, in freefall, thinking about how they're going to land
5. Fall (contact pose)
6. Recovery pose
7. Neutral pose

SOMETIMES IT IS THE PEOPLE NO ONE IMAGINES ANYTHING OF WHO DO THE THINGS THAT NO ONE CAN IMAGINE.

ALAN TURING (1912–1954)

Turing was a mathematician with a brilliant mind. As well as helping crack the Enigma code in World War II, in 1936 he published a paper that would become the foundation of computer science. Observing the step-by-step process a person would follow to complete a task, he invented the idea of a "universal machine" that could decode and perform a set of instructions: algorithms. Ten years later, Turing produced a practical plan for an electronic computer called the Automatic Computing Engine, which could run these programs and store them in its memory.

THE MATH BEHIND THE REALISM

Computer animation has come a long way since its origins in the 1960s. These days, it can be hard to tell what's real and what's not. Animators use computer programs and 3D effects, harnessing the principles of geometry, calculus, and algebra to add that special touch of realism. Here are two examples of how it's done:

• Transforming a 2D object into 3D uses geometry, mapping, and coordinates.

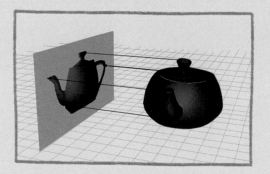

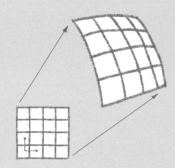

DID YOU KNOW?

The first computer-generated animation was of a cat. It was created by mathematician Nikolai Konstantinov.

• Variety is essential to making something look natural. This is created by changing some parameters while keeping others constant.

Right Plenty of variables: the number, distributions, color, length, and curve of each blade.

Wrong Each blade of grass is completely identical.

BOWLED OVER BY MATH

Calculus is the study of how things change over time. Newton's laws of motion help us understand how things behave when they are still, when they are moving, and what forces act upon them. All of this comes into play when you go bowling, where the aim is to roll a heavy ball down a wooden lane and knock over all ten pins. Here we look at the numbers and equations behind the perfect strike.

BOWLING BALL

Bowling balls are made from resin. They have a smooth surface with three finger holes. One of the most critical elements in bowling is the speed of the bowling ball, which is affected by its weight and by its special core, which provides spin and momentum.

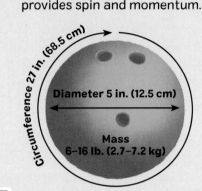

Circumference 27 in. (68.5 cm)

Diameter 5 in. (12.5 cm)

Mass
6–16 lb. (2.7–7.2 kg)

TEN-PIN BOWLING IN NUMBERS

3.3–3.5 lb. (1.5–1.6kg) The mass of a pin

3 equal sides—the pins are arranged in an equilateral triangle formation

12 in. (30 cm) the space between each pin

30 The number of points for a strike

15 cm (38 cm) The height of a pin, which is also the circumference of its belly

300 The maximum number of points possible in a perfect game

VELOCITY VS. SPEED

Speed is a measurement of how fast something is moving. It is a scalar measurement, which means it represents size.

$$\text{speed} = \frac{\text{distance}}{\text{time}}$$

Velocity is also a measurement of how fast something is moving, but it has direction as well as magnitude, making it a vector measurement.

$$\text{velocity} = \frac{\text{displacement}}{\text{time}}$$

Displacement is the distance moved in a straight line, or a given direction from a starting point

Momentum is the force going in the ball's favor.

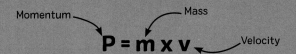

Momentum ⟶

Mass ⟶

$$P = m \times v$$

⟵ Velocity

For example, if your bowling ball has a mass of 6 lb., and its average velocity is 24.5 ft./sec.,

then its momentum = **6 x 24.5 = 147 lb. ft./sec.**

Friction

Momentum

Friction will slow down the course of the ball. How much it slows depends on the smoothness and mass of the ball and the smoothness of the lane. Some friction is useful in a throw—a bowler needs to find the perfect balance.

The equation for kinetic friction is as follows:

$$F_k = mg\,\mu k$$

Force due to kinetic friction ⟶

Mass of the ball ⟶ ⟵ Gravity

⟵ Coefficient of kinetic friction

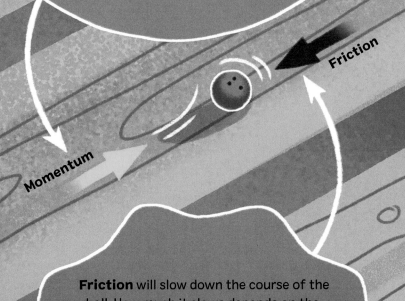

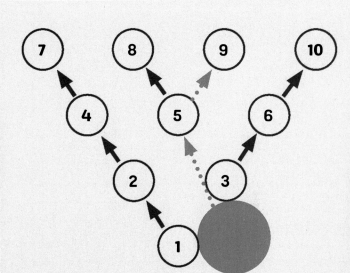

THE MATH OF A PERFECT STRIKE

Scoring a perfect strike is a combination of using the best bowling speed and hitting the pins at the right angle.

An entry angle of 4–6° is considered the most successful, while the best bowling speed is 21 mph at release point and 17 mph at strike point.

For a bowling lane of 60 ft., how long should it take between release and strike point to hit the recommended average speed of 16.7 mph (24.5 feet per second)?

Here's how can you work it out:

1. Rearrange the speed equation so that:

$$\text{Time} = \frac{\text{displacement}}{\text{average speed}}$$

2. Slot the numbers into the equation:

$$\text{Time} = \frac{60}{24.5} = 2.5 \text{ seconds}$$

THE MATH OF LIVING

The cost of living affects everyone. Being able to balance the books—recording how much money is coming in against how much is going out—is a key factor in staying out of debt. Add to that a good understanding of interest, inflation, and how tax works, and you will have a sound understanding of good money management. Here are some of the equations involved.

BALANCING THE BOOKS

Equations don't have to be complicated to be helpful!

Net income = income – expenses

Good budgeting should help you make sure your income is bigger than your expenses.

INCOME

This is the money you have coming in. It could be from pocket money or part-time job earnings, or even from the interest paid on your savings. Interest is the cost of borrowing money—a bank will pay you interest on your savings because you are lending them your money. The interest rate is the amount of interest due to be paid to you in a set time period. There are two main ways to calculate it:

1. Simple interest

Interest = amount invested x rate of interest x time

If you invest **$1,000** with an interest rate of **10%** over 1 year, the interest earned would be:

Interest = $1,000 x 0.10 x 1 = $100
After the 1st year, your savings will have grown to **$1,100**.

However, what this equation doesn't factor in is the interest you earn on interest earned. That's where compound interest comes in.

2. Compound interest

Compound interest calculates interest on the interest earned as well as the original amount that was invested. It can be calculated using:

New value ↴   ↳ Number of years.

$$V = I \times (1 + r)^n$$

Original investment ↗   ↖ Annual rate of interest (as a decimal)

Imagine you decide to save your money for three years. Using the simple interest equation, you'd get:

Interest = $1,000 x 0.10 x 3 = $300
meaning your savings would grow to **$1,300**.

But if we factor in the compound interest we get **V = $1,000 x (1 + 0.10)³ = $1,331**

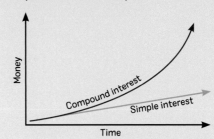

Money

Compound interest

Simple interest

Time

34

EXPENSES

These are the ways we spend money, from smaller purchases such as clothes and food to larger ones, such as buying a house. Debt is a deferred payment of something using financial tools such as credit cards and loans. Not all debt is bad. Mortgages enable people to buy high-value things such as homes and spread the cost over a long period of time, to make it affordable.

HOW TAX WORKS

Tax is a compulsory financial charge that enables a government to fund spending. Income tax is a proportion of your earnings. Understanding what impact it has on your own income is a valuable skill to have.

Earnings	Example tax due
Up to 10,000	0%
10,000 – 20,000	10%
20,000 – 30,000	20%
30,000 +	30%

ANNUAL PERCENTAGE RATE

When you borrow money, you agree to pay the loan back over a set period of time, with fixed monthly repayments. Annual percentage rate (APR) is the yearly amount it will cost you to pay back the interest on your loan.

The key things to know when taking out a loan are:

• **What are the monthly payments?**

• **How much interest you will pay over time?**

• **What is the total amount you will repay (loan plus interest)?**

Then ask yourself:

• **Can you afford it, and is it worth it?!**

HOW INFLATION WORKS

Inflation is a steady rise in prices. It means that your money today won't buy you quite as much as it did yesterday.

How inflation has changed the price of a cup of coffee over time

1980	1990	2000	2010	2022
$0.45	$0.75	$1.00	$1.25	$1.85

THE MATH IN MOTORSPORTS

Ever since the invention of the gasoline-fueled internal combustion engine in the 1880s, thrill-seeking individuals have been willing to compete in cross-country road races and long-distance endurance courses. Drive, innovation, and the development of racecourses have furthered the pursuit of high speeds. To push these boundaries safely requires design, mechanics, and talent—and to do all that, you need math.

SPEED

A racing team will want to measure the speed of a car. There are two ways to do this:

1. Average speed

This is the speed at which the car travels on average, over the course of its whole drive.

$$\text{Speed} = \frac{\text{distance}}{\text{time}}$$

2. Instantaneous speed

This is the fastest that the car travels at the one absolute fastest moment in its drive. It's faster than the average speed!

DID YOU KNOW?

The first organized race took place in 1894. It was in France, from Paris to Rouen, and was won with an average speed of 10.2 mph (16.4 kmh)!

THE NEED FOR SPEED

Driving fast relies on the terrain of a course; the power, aerodynamics, and technology of a car; and the talent of the drivers, who must judge the latest possible moment to brake on corners. Here are some of the top speeds in motorsports:

	Top speed	Acceleration
Formula 1	223 mph / 360 kmh	0–60 mph in 2.6 sec.
Indy Car	236 mph / 380 kmh	0–62 mph in 3 sec.
NASCAR	199 mph / 321 kmh	0–60 mph in 3.4 sec.
Formula 2	208 mph / 335 kmh	0–62 mph in 2.9 sec.
Formula 3	186 mph / 300 kmh	0–62 mph in 3.1 sec.
Formula E	174 mph / 280 kmh	0–62 mph in 2.8 sec.

AERODYNAMICS

Racecars are designed and built using CAD (computer-aided design) to produce complex 3D drawings. One of the most important considerations is aerodynamics. Fluid dynamics studies the flow of fluids and gases and how forces affect them. Designers utilize the downforce (vertical load) created by the aerodynamic parts when the car is in motion, to push it down, increasing grip and stability.

A higher downforce makes a car faster on tight corners but will lessen its overall speed.

BERNOULLI'S PRINCIPLE

Gases and fluids moving at high speeds will have lower pressure than those moving at low speeds. This is the principle behind how planes can fly, and it can also be applied to racecars to keep them on the ground.

$$\text{Pressure} = \frac{\text{force}}{\text{area}}$$

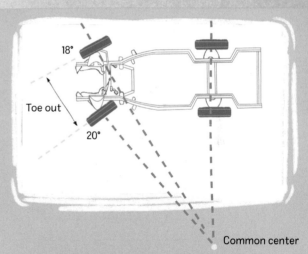

18°

Toe out

20°

Common center

ACKERMANN STEERING GEOMETRY

Steering geometry is used to maximize the performance of a car's tires. Represented as a percentage, the Ackermann steering angle is the configuration that allows both front wheels to be steered at appropriate angles to avoid tire sliding. Most cars aren't run on 100% Ackermann but are fine-tuned according to the speed and track where the car is racing. The slower and tighter the track, the more the designer will use Ackermann angles to navigate hairpins and other tight corners.

SHAPES IN SPACE

To officially become an astronaut, a person must travel above the boundary between Earth's atmosphere and space. NASA classifies this as 50 mi. (80.5 km) above sea level, while others use the Kármán Line, at 62 mi. (100 km) above sea level. Regardless of who is right, building a rocket with enough thrust to get out of Earth's atmosphere is one of humanity's greatest achievements. It was only possible thanks to technology, math, and some brilliant minds.

Quadratic equations are used to solve problems in motion. They take the standard form:

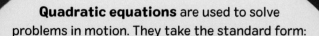

This makes the equation quadratic

$$ax^2 + bx + c = 0$$

x is an unknown variable

a, b, and c are known coefficients.

THE MATH OF LIFTOFF

How much acceleration does a rocket need to take off? We can rearrange the equation for Newton's second law of motion to find out. Newton's second law states:

Force → Mass →

$$F = m\, a$$

Acceleration ↵

First, we rearrange: $a = F / m$

Then we can rewrite force as $F = T - W$

The equation then becomes:

$$a = \frac{T - W}{m}$$

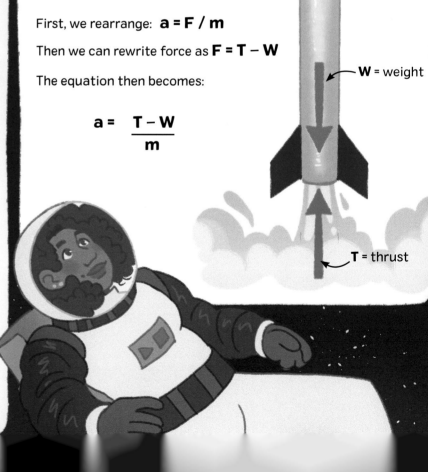

W = weight

T = thrust

BARBARA CANRIGHT (1919–1997)

Canright was the first female mathematician to be hired by NASA's Jet Propulsion Laboratory (JPL). Before computers were available, teams of people were required to carry out long and complex calculations using only pencil, paper, and a slide rule. At a time when most women could only be secretaries, teachers, or nurses, JPL had a computer room full of female computers. It was the calculations of these women that made the first rockets possible. Canright was instrumental in calculating thrust-to-weight ratio, comparing the performance of engines under different conditions.

THE SHAPE OF MOTION

After liftoff, a rocket becomes a projectile (a moving object with only the force of gravity acting upon it). The path the rocket follows through space is called its trajectory. If velocity describes the direction and speed of motion, then a trajectory describes the shape of it.

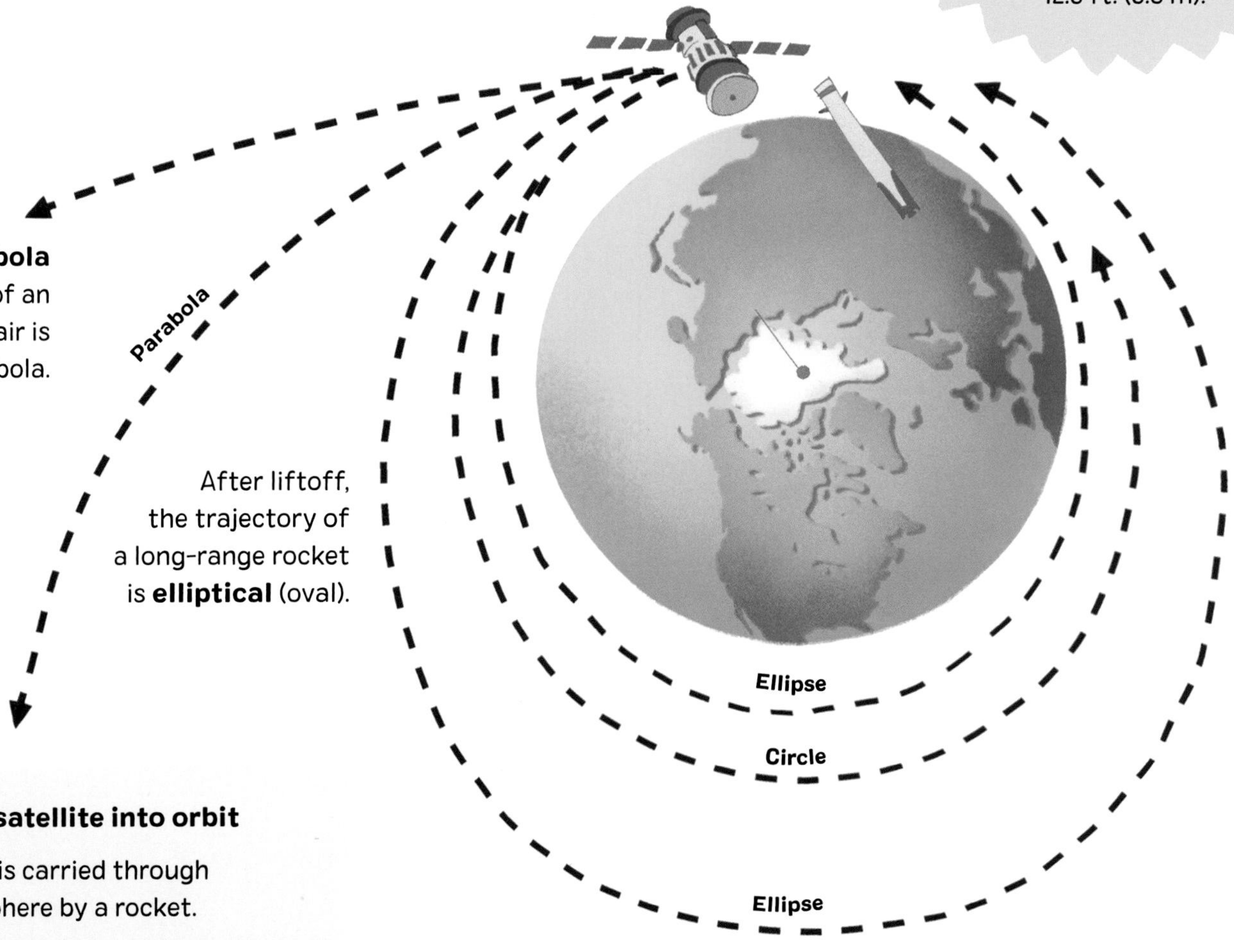

Parabola
The path of an object in the air is a parabola.

Parabola

After liftoff, the trajectory of a long-range rocket is **elliptical** (oval).

Ellipse

Circle

Ellipse

How to get a satellite into orbit

1. The satellite is carried through Earth's atmosphere by a rocket.

2. The rocket sends the satellite into orbit at a very precise speed. If it were too slow, it would fall to Earth, while if it were too fast, it would escape Earth's orbit.

An **orbit** is the repeated path an object follows around another object, because of gravity. The Sun has eight planets, including Earth, whose orbits around it are almost circular.

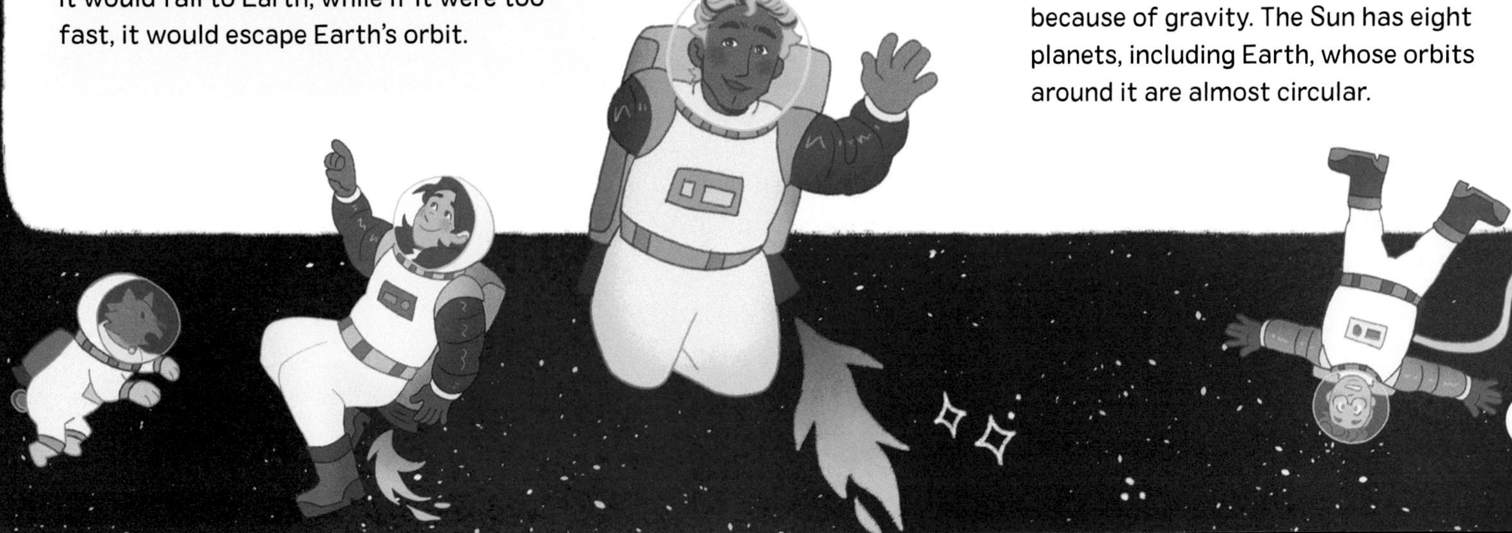

READY...AIM...FIRE!

Newton's laws of motion help us understand the behavior of an object at rest or when moving, as well as the forces that can change this. Here's your chance to put these laws into action by building your own catapult and then experimenting with launching different objects from it.

WARNING:

Have an adult supervise!

YOU WILL NEED
- Large rubber bands
- Six 3 ft. (1 m) bamboo canes
- A paper cup
- Scissors
- Small objects such as a table tennis ball, pebble, marshmallow, and cork

INSTRUCTIONS

1. Build the triangular base of the catapult by making three bamboo canes into a triangle and securing them with rubber bands.

2. Turn your triangle into a pyramid by attaching the other three canes. One cane will attach to each corner of the triangle. Secure them at the apex of the pyramid with more rubber bands.

3. Make three evenly spaced holes around the rim of the paper cup.

4. Cut three rubber bands in half. Thread each of them through one of the holes in the cup and make a knot to hold it in place.

5. Tie the loose ends of the rubber bands to the corners of one of the faces of your pyramid structure.

6. Put an object in the cup, pull it back, take aim, and fire!

40

THE NEED FOR SPEED

Now that you've got a working catapult, you can use it to run some experiments. Let's assess which object travels the farthest and which the fastest. Speed is the rate of change of distance, and it is calculated using the following equation:

Distance traveled

$$S = d / t$$

Speed

Time

1. Make a prediction. Which object do you think will travel the farthest? Is it the heaviest or the lightest? Which object will travel the fastest?

2. Now put your theories to the test. Lay the extra stick on the ground. This is your starting line, where you will rest the front of your catapult. Decide which direction you are firing in and try to maintain it throughout the experiment. Likewise, try to pull the catapult cup back the same distance each time, so that you are exerting the same force on each object.

3. Have your friend start the timer the moment you fire each object. They could guide you on when to fire, saying "ready, aim, fire!" They need to stop the timer the moment your object comes to rest.

4. Measure how far each object travels.

5. Using the equation s = d/t, figure out the speed at which each object traveled.

6. Now compare notes for each object. Did your predictions come true?

THE TASTE OF SWEET SUCCESS

YOU WILL NEED
- Two large bags of candy
- Pen and paper to record your findings

Have you ever thought that there's always more of one color in a bag of candy than of the others? Well, here's an experiment to test if your hunch is right.

METHOD

1. Make a prediction. Which do you think the most common color will be?

2. Open one pack (don't eat them!).

3. Count the total number of candies, then split them into individual colors and record the total number of each.

4. Figure out the percentages of each color using this formula:

$$100 \times \frac{\text{total no. of color}}{\text{total no. of sweets}}$$

5. Which is the most common color? Did it match your prediction?

6. Now open another pack and do the experiment again. Does it give you the same answer?

	Green	Orange	Yellow	Red	Purple
Total number of candies					
% of total					

PARTY TRICKS

Ever wanted to impress your guests with a mind-reading party trick? Here are two ways to do it, using just a calculator and some algebra.

YOUR TURN!

YOU WILL NEED
• A calculator
• A willing victim
• A magician's hat if you want the full effect

MIND-READING NUMBERS

1. Write the number 1 on a piece of paper and then fold it up, to be opened later.

2. Ask your victim to pick a number, any number.

3. Add 3 to that number, then double the result.

4. Subtract 4, then halve the result.

5. Subtract the original number.

6. Now open the folded piece of paper to reveal the answer. It will be correct, because the answer is always 1!

7. As an extra challenge, can you write an equation that shows what's happening here? Use "n" to represent the number your victim chooses.

GUESS SOMEONE'S BIRTHDAY

For this trick, your victim will operate the calculator. All you have to do is give them the operations to input and rub your temples throughout as if you are mind reading. Your victim will need to press "equals" at the end of each step.

1. Ask them to input the day (two digits) of their birthday.

2. Add 15.

3. Now multiply by 25.

4. Minus 321.

5. Multiply by 8.

6. Minus 554.

7. Divide by 2.

8. Ask them to add the month of their birthday, as two digits.

9. Now multiply by 5.

10. Add 692.

11. Multiply by 20.

12. Add their birthday year, as two digits.

13. Minus 7,740.

14. The digits of their birthday will appear on the calculator. Ta da!

ANSWER
This method produces this equation:

$$\frac{(n+3) \times 2 - 4}{2} - n = n + 3 - 2 - n = n + 1 - n = 1$$

ESTIMATE THE HEIGHT OF A TREE

YOUR TURN!

YOU WILL NEED
- A friend
- A pencil
- A tape measure

You don't need an enormous ruler to measure something tall. Here are two ways you can measure a tree using something as simple as a pencil!

1. USING MEASUREMENTS

INSTRUCTIONS

1. Get your friend to stand next to the tree you want to measure.

2. Hold your pencil up vertically, and move away from the tree until the pencil looks like it is the same size as the tree.

3. Don't move! Rotate your pencil to horizontal, so that one end looks like it is touching the tree trunk.

4. Ask your friend to move away from the tree until they look like they are at the opposite end of the pencil.

5. Now measure the distance between the tree trunk and your friend. This is the height of the tree!

44

2. USING THE PROPERTIES OF SIMILAR TRIANGLES

YOU WILL NEED
• A pencil
• A tree with space around it and a trunk that has a right angle with the ground
• The Sun

INSTRUCTIONS

1 Place your pencil vertically on the ground, making sure that it is at a right angle to the ground.

2 Measure the height of the pencil and the length of its shadow.

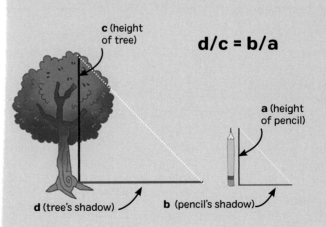

3 Immediately measure the length of the tree's shadow.

WHAT'S GOING ON?

These two triangles are similar—they both have right angles. This means that we can use the equation for similar triangles to compare them and find out missing lengths:

4 Now for some math:

$$\frac{\text{Length of tree shadow}}{\text{Height of tree}} = \frac{\text{Length of pencil shadow}}{\text{Height of pencil}}$$

We can rearrange the equation to find the height of the tree:

$$\text{Height of tree} = \frac{\text{Length of tree shadow} \times \text{Height of pencil}}{\text{Length of pencil shadow}}$$

What answer do you get?

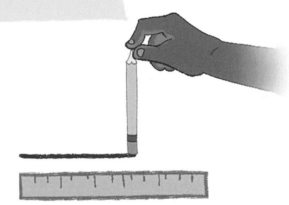

c (height of tree)

d/c = b/a

a (height of pencil)

d (tree's shadow)

b (pencil's shadow)

GLOSSARY

Atmosphere
The layer of air that surrounds a star or planet. Beyond the atmosphere is space.

Aerodynamics
The study of the way that objects move through air and interact with it.

Enigma code
A difficult-to-crack code used by Germany during World War II to send top-secret messages.

Friction
The force that acts when objects or surfaces rub against each other, slowing them down and providing grip.

Geometry
The branch of math that deals with shapes: points, lines, angles, and surfaces, and the relationships between them.

GPS
Global Positioning System—our phones and other GPS devices use information sent by satellites around Earth to tell us exactly where we are.

Gravity
The force pulling objects toward each other or down to the ground.

Hypotenuse
The longest side of a right triangle, the side opposite the right angle.

Income
The amount of money received by an individual or organization.

Income tax
A payment to the government consisting of part of a person's income, compulsory in most countries.

Interest
Money a lender receives for lending out money or a borrower pays for borrowing it.

Kinetic energy
Moving energy. All moving objects have kinetic energy.

Metrology
The science of measurement.

Momentum
A measure of the "oomph" that an object has; its movement. Momentum is mass multiplied by velocity.

Newton's third law
The law that states that whenever two objects meet, they apply equal and opposite forces on each other. Sometimes expressed as "every action has an equal and opposite reaction."

Satellite
An object that revolves around a larger object in space. Moons are natural satellites. Artificial satellites include communications satellites, which orbit Earth.

Statistics
A branch of math that deals with collecting and analyzing data.

Symmetry
A property of a 2D or 3D shape meaning it remains the same if you transform it by reflecting or rotating it.

Tessellation
A pattern of repeated 2D shapes that fit together without any gaps.

Time zone
A region where the same standard time is used.

Trigonometry
A branch of math that deals with the relationship between the sides and angles of triangles.

Variable
An unknown number in an equation.

WiFi
A wireless networking technology that uses radio waves to send data at high speeds over short distances. Stands for "wireless fidelity."

Zenith
The highest point in the celestial sphere, or the point directly above the observer.

Picture credits
The Publisher would like to thank the following for permission to reproduce their material.
5b: Vyychan/Dreamstime

INDEX

THE AUTHOR & ILLUSTRATOR

LOU ABERCROMBIE

Lou has always loved numbers. She studied at Durham University in England, where she gained a first-class BS degree in mathematics. She now writes fiction and nonfiction books for children and hopes to inspire others to share her passion by celebrating the creativity that can be found within the subject. Lou is also a photographer and enthusiastic wild swimmer. She lives in Bath with her husband, fantasy novelist Joe Abercrombie, and their three children.

@LadyGrimdark
www.louabercrombie.com

EVELYN ROGERS

Evelyn Rogers is an American children's book illustrator who lives in California. They began drawing at a young age, making all sorts of things inspired by graphic novels, classic children's books, superhero comics, and fantasy novels. When Evelyn isn't drawing, they can be found performing on stage, sewing a new costume, or cuddling their cat and dog.